HOUSING ≡ FOR ≡ PURPOSE

AF076401

HOUSING FOR PURPOSE

A Guide to Investing in Real Estate for Both Profit and Social Good

Whitney Sellers

gatekeeper press
Where Authors are Family
Columbus, Ohio

The views and opinions expressed in this book are solely those of the author and do not reflect the views or opinions of Gatekeeper Press. Gatekeeper Press is not to be held responsible for and expressly disclaims responsibility of the content herein.

Housing For Purpose: A Guide to Investing in Real Estate for Both Profit and Social Good

Published by Gatekeeper Press
2167 Stringtown Rd, Suite 109
Columbus, OH 43123-2989
www.GatekeeperPress.com

Copyright © 2022 by Whitney Chaffin-Sellers
All rights reserved. Neither this book, nor any parts within it may be sold or reproduced in any form or by any electronic or mechanical means, including information storage and retrieval systems, without permission in writing from the author. The only exception is by a reviewer, who may quote short excerpts in a review.

Library of Congress Control Number: 2022943920

ISBN (paperback): 9781662931321
eISBN: 9781662931338

Disclaimer

All information contained herein is strictly limited to informational and educational purposes only, and some is from the perspective and opinion of the author. There are no cited sources in this book, as the author wrote it off the top of her head one day in her living room. Everything within this book was either something learned or experienced firsthand.

All information contained herein should not be construed as legal, tax, or specific investment advice. Each person's situation is unique. Always consult with a knowledgeable advisor and attorney before making investment, business, tax, or financial decisions.

This book provides information and provides no guarantees, promises, representations, or warranties of any kind regarding specific general benefits, monetary or otherwise, from Whitney Sellers, Whitney's Place, Elite Legacy Education, Inc., Place of Hope, or affiliated partners. These entities are not responsible for and shall not be held liable for anything written in this book or for any investment and/or business success or failure, acts or commissions, the appropriateness of the reader's decisions, or the use of reliance on this information.

Investing in real estate and/or business does involve risk. It always involves risk. Entrepreneurs and investors can both make and lose money on any given transaction. Like the stock market, poor decisions may result in the loss of all or part of an individual's working capital. Always invest with caution after consulting with your attorney and accountant on your personal risk tolerance.

This information is not to be construed as a security offering of any kind. Prior to making any decisions to contribute capital to anything related to or involving Whitney Chaffin Sellers, investors must review and execute all private offering documents, including any project prospectus and private placement memorandum. Access to information about any investment is limited to investors who qualify as accredited investors within the meaning of the Securities Act of 1933, as amended, and Rule 501 of Regulation D, circulated there from.

Table of Contents

Introduction ix

Chapter 1 What Is Housing for Purpose? 1
Advantages and Disadvantages 2
Populations We Serve 5
Types of Specialized Housing 6

Chapter 2 The Importance of Housing as a
Social Good 11
Building Sustainable Communities 14
Diversity Promotion 15

Chapter 3 Building a Legacy 17
Figuring Out Your Why 18

Chapter 4 Introduction to Real Estate
Investing 21
Common Questions 25

Chapter 5	Housing as a Business 27
	Types of Properties...............................28
	Purchasing a Property 30
	How Do We Make Money?...................31
Chapter 6	Housing Requirements..........................35
Chapter 7	The Details...37
	Tricks of the Trade................................40
Chapter 8	Network for Net Worth........................41
	Who Is on Your Power Team? 41
Chapter 9	Marketing Your Mission 45
Chapter 10	The Power of Giving Back 53
	Providing Second Chances 56
	Making a Difference 63
	Leaving a Legacy...................................65

Conclusion 67
Action Plan 69
Contact Information 70

Introduction

Have you ever wanted to make money? Have you ever wanted to help people? Have you ever thought about how you can do both?

My name is Whitney Sellers, formerly Whitney Chaffin, and I love to make money, but more importantly, I love to help people. What I've learned through the years is that money is just a tool that can give me the ability to help people on a grander scale.

I grew up having a burning desire to give back to others, but I always thought I had to have a lot of money to do so. What if I told you that giving back is exactly how to get the money, or at least, how you put yourself in a position to make the money you've always dreamed of? That's my belief, at least.

See, saving your way to wealth to one day be able to give some of it away seems like a very long, risky process, and there are no guarantees in life except for death. Any of us could be gone tomorrow, and you can't take anything with you, so why not do all the good things you want to do while you still have time? Is money what's holding you back?

Let's first look at money: We live in a world now where paper money has basically become obsolete. Think about the last time you used cash, or coins, or took money out of an ATM. Think about all the new digital currencies out there. There are books and articles from years and years ago explaining the value of the dollar and how it's been devalued overtime and how because of this, saving your way to wealth is nearly impossible. The new way to flaunt wealth is by buying assets that can make you money—such as real estate. And in my opinion, your wealth is determined not only by financial gain and net worth, but also by how many people's lives you can change from your actions.

Let's now look at real estate: Housing is the *new* currency, representing 163 trillion dollars of global wealth, or nearly three times the world GDP. Although real estate has been around since the history of time (caves), I say *new* currency because there has recently been a shift in the way we view real estate or housing specifically. Housing as a commodity has usurped the traditional purpose of housing: shelter, protection, and housing provision. Four walls and a ceiling are now rough terms for the dollar sign.

While some people may make huge profits from land appreciation and rising property values, for many people around the world, especially right now, the downside is a severe lack of accessibility and inventory, mass evictions and foreclosures, great inequality, and eventual homelessness or bankruptcy, depending on what side of the coin you're on. With the support of the free market, free from financial rules, housing has become an important wealth vehicle because everyone on earth—good or bad, happy or sad, mean or nice—needs a place to rest their head at night.

Right now, the world is up in arms about the housing market. People are leaving states they grew up in and have lived in their entire lives to move to places with fewer restrictions, both politically and legally. The demand and prices of real estate are going up, while the inventory supply is going down. The disruptive nature of relocating is not limited to developing nations and foreclosures as in previous years. It has spread worldwide due to a lack of regulations to curb the growing trend of treating housing as a financial asset without worrying about keeping housing as a social asset.

Foreclosures, distressed situations—all of those things can put someone out of their home, but what about people who are already homeless? What about our vulnerable populations? What about homeless veterans? What about homeless children? What about men and women who are in active addiction and desperately want to get their life back but don't have a safe place to live?

Housing for purpose is a way we can solve a major problem—we can provide safe and sustainable housing to people who need a second chance to truly get their life back, and we can do so in a way that is mutually beneficial.

CHAPTER 1

What Is Housing for Purpose?

Housing for purpose is a real estate investment strategy in which housing is provided by owners or housing associations (non-profit organizations that own, rent, and manage rental housing) or the local city council to do a good deed that impacts society in a positive way. *Housing for purpose* is an interchangeable term with *social housing, municipal housing,* or even the term *co-housing or shared housing*; however, these types of housing differ slightly in terms of the type of lease you sign and the rights you have over the property accordingly. We describe these a little later in the chapter.

The idea behind this type of housing is that you can change lives while making a profit, usually a higher profit than a traditional rental property. Don't get me wrong—traditional rentals are great, but what if you could rent to multiple people under one roof who need help getting back on their feet? Not only could you be making a higher cash flow and overall profit by having more residents paying rent, but you'd be able to provide a safe place for people to build themselves up again, in a healthy and accepting environment.

Advantages and Disadvantages

Advantages for the residents:

- It can be cheaper than private rent for the individual renter.
- The properties are typically in greater condition for a fraction of the cost.
- It can provide a better support system for the individual's progress, since individuals will be living among a supportive peer group in similar situations.
- It typically provides a safer, long-term rental for people of vulnerable populations.
- It gives the residents greater rights and greater control over their homes and mental health, and the opportunity to be better can take root.

Advantages for the investors:

- It can provide higher returns on investments (ROIs) to the homeowner/investor resulting in higher cash flow.

- It can lower vacancy rates, since you're renting to multiple people and since the individuals you house usually have fewer affordable and safe housing options, so they're less likely to move out.
- It can be a secure source of income when third-party groups are involved with rental financial assistance, as there are grants, subsidies, and funding available.
- It can allow for you to give back to others in a greater way by your participation in the individual's recovery or comeback.
- Depending on how your business is structured, you may have additional tax benefits you can tap into (must consult with your attorney and CPA on this).
- You may also be able to receive donations or start-up cost assistance.
- As an investor, you have more structured tenants who are used to being held accountable for their actions.
- At the end of the day, you're helping people recover in a safe environment.

Disadvantages for the residents:

- Residents may have to share a room.

- There may be a lack of availability.
- They will need to trust in your housing model, as there are a lot of scammers out there who don't put the residents' needs first.
- Multiple personalities under one roof may clash.
- Rental assistance doesn't last forever.

Disadvantages for the investor:

- We can't save everyone.
- Timeframe to fill a property with residents in the home sometimes takes longer than a traditional renter.
- Requires educating the public, as you may get neighborhood pushback.
- Takes longer to build the business system.
- More restrictions (in some cases)
- Turnover (not typical vacancies)
- Not every county/city/state has same requirements/restrictions, which requires lots of due diligence.
- There are more rules and regulations to be aware of.
- Local restrictions
- Can be management intensive.

Right now, we are facing a national housing emergency. Successive governments have failed to provide the stable, good-quality social housing that people need, leaving millions of people isolated and struggling to find a safe home. Therefore, we push for governments (and investors) to invest in a new generation of social housing. Social housing rent is cheaper when compared to private sector rent. The increase in rent is also sometimes limited by local governments, which means that homes must remain affordable over the long term so that people in their communities are not overpriced due to the higher rent.

Populations We Serve

Anyone can live in a shared housing environment, as this strategy can extend into student housing or even short-term rentals, but most social housing populations are people who have a special need. Eligibility is based on housing needs, organizations you're working with, and desire. Typically, the vulnerable populations we focus on are anyone experiencing homelessness, including the following:

- Veterans
- People with mental and/or physical disabilities, including addiction and PTSD

- Victims of domestic violence, sexual abuse, or human trafficking
- Children aging out of foster care
- Re-entry/Returning citizens from prison who are in transition back into society
- Those needing assisted living services
- People in drug and alcohol recovery who need clean and sober housing
- Neglected children, foster children, and young adults aging out of the foster care system
- Homeless people
- Troubled youth
- LGBTQIA population

(This list is ongoing, and there is no one-size-fits-all when it comes to the populations who need help. If you have a special group you want to house, I'm certain it can be done.)

Types of Specialized Housing

- **Social Good Housing**: Low rent (usually 50–60 percent of market rent), usually renting a room or a bed, safe and clean and sometimes program-based.

What Is Housing for Purpose?

- **Affordable Rental Housing:** Higher-rent housing (typically up to 80 percent of market rent) and less secure housing, organized as needed through government assistance such as Section 8.
- **Shared Housing:** To partially rent a home, either by room or by bed, or by day versus month. (AirBnB, VRBO, student housing—this book does not detail the general co-housing model, but we do offer courses and materials on this.)
- **Assisted Living:** For people with additional needs, such as nursing homes; however, there is a difference between a nursing home and assisted living facility in many areas.

Within each type of specialized housing, there are several levels which allow for you to decide on your level of involvement. Do you want to be involved in the residents' lives? Or would you rather be completely hands-off? There are ways you can do either or both, but it requires a better understanding of your state, city, and county laws, rules, regulations, requirements, and restrictions.

A great resource to better understand your local requirements would be your local building department and zoning division.

Currently, the law establishes who is entitled to social housing and who should take preference. But city councils have a lot of flexibility regarding who is entitled locally, and social owners can refuse to let people in if they wish.

There are currently hundreds of thousands of people who are homeless and in need of a safe place to live, which means there is a huge opportunity for private investors to help those in need.

Unfortunately, the chronic shortage of housing means there is not enough housing for people in urgent need, such as homeless people currently living on the street and homeless families with young children, or people released from prison, which happens on a regular basis.

We believe that high-quality social housing should be available to all who need it, including families and the homeless, private tenants in need, and others who cannot find adequate housing. People who live in social houses tend to have secure leases, since sometimes the individuals can't qualify to live in homes that require a more extensive qualification process, so this can provide much greater protection against eviction with improved rights than private tenants. This means people can take root, plan, and make their home a home.

What Is Housing for Purpose?

On average, the houses we use to provide for the vulnerable populations are more likely to meet "decent" housing standards. They are better insulated, more energy-efficient, and are more likely to have working smoke detectors than other types of homes. Investments in home maintenance and improvement have been patchy over the years, but the mission with social housing is to have nice houses in good neighborhoods close to public transportation and things to do.

EXERCISE: Mapping Out Your "Why" and Motivation

Answer the following:

1. Why social housing?
2. What groups are you wanting to help?
3. What is it that interests you about it?
4. Set a goal and put a date on it.

"I will _____ by _____ so that I can _____. It's important to me because _____."

CHAPTER 2

The Importance of Housing as a Social Good

When we are born into this world, we don't think about housing or the affordability of it until we reach adulthood; at least, that's the reality for most people. But some people face housing insecurity through their parents from the time they are born. Whether we individually experience it or not, decent and affordable housing is important for families, and particularly important for our most vulnerable populations.

Housing not only satisfies a basic human need for shelter, but it also contributes to the well-being of human life. Studies show that children in stable housing excel in school and are less likely to be interrupted by unwanted movements. Decent and affordable housing reduces stress, leading to better physical and mental health.

Let's take, for example, someone returning to society from prison. Yes, he or she may have committed a crime—I understand that. So sometimes, the first thought is "Why do they deserve a nice house?" But what if that individual was convicted of a non-violent crime, such as selling marijuana across state lines? I'm not condoning it and not making it political, but think for a second about that. That person did their time for their crime of selling a drug that is now legal in many states. And in many cases, it costs the states thousands of dollars that taxpayers pay to keep people incarcerated for non-violent crimes. If someone is returning to society from prison, he or she may not have the financial ability to afford housing, to spend on health care and food and other necessities. Not only that, but he or she may not have a safe place to live, which then can lead to another problem called recidivism. Having an affordable place to live in a safe neighborhood can truly change someone's life for the better and contribute to closing the gap on how many people return to prison after release.

Research has also shown that children whose parents receive housing assistance benefit from better nutrition than those who need it and don't have it. Affordable housing is essential for the economic vitality of communities. On the surface, it can be a competitive advantage for local employers because it can help the local workforce so they can live close to their work. Shorter commutes allow workers to spend adequate time with their families, while the community benefits from reduced traffic, air pollution, and road costs. By revitalizing communities, building affordable housing can also help stimulate economic growth.

A healthy mix of housing options, from market-priced and affordable rental homes, single-family and duplex homes, and senior citizen developments, provides opportunities for all people to improve their economic situation and contribute to their communities. The needs of your community are important. Houses for rent meet the needs of many families who cannot qualify to purchase a home. For some, particularly low- and middle-income families in high-cost markets, or families who have recently lost a home due to foreclosure, renting a home is the most financially realistic option.

For some families, affordable rental accommodation is an important starting point to accumulate savings and prepare for homeownership. Homeownership is also an essential part of real estate and can be a durable and affordable option when mortgage terms and home prices are within the family's budget. For many working families, homeownership is the American dream; in addition to being your greatest financial asset, homeownership provides security against unwanted control over the functions of your home. Research has shown that homeownership is beneficial for children: they are more likely to do well in school, less likely to have behavioral problems, and less likely to become pregnant in their teens. From a community perspective, homeowners can stabilize the neighborhoods in which they invest. For these reasons, communities should strive to ensure that there are enough rental and residential units to meet the substantial needs of all families in the community.

We believe that affordable housing is not a helping hand; it's a hand up. It allows families to reimagine their future and build a legacy they're proud of.

Building Sustainable Communities

The need for affordable housing is essential, not only for families who depend on housing but also for the surrounding communities. By working with city governments, housing organizations, and community advocates, you can create communities in which families can thrive. Studies have shown that affordable housing raises the population level, enhances social contact, reduces overcrowding, increases the value of neighboring properties, attracts businesses and jobs, and reduces crime rates. There are many economic benefits to affordable housing, such as rising expenditures, increased employment, and increased taxes and revenue to local governments. When families and individuals who have experienced hardship can worry less about rent, those who live in affordable housing can spend more on nutritious foods and other necessities. Increasing the purchasing power of low-income families can mean steady income for local businesses, more job creation, and economic growth.

Diversity Promotion

Affordable housing development promotes diversity by creating communities in which people from diverse cultural, social, economic, and educational backgrounds can come together. Different societies raise awareness of cultural sensitivity, equality, and understanding of different backgrounds, which ultimately leads to a better inclusive society. Investments in community building help diverse neighbors overcome their fears and doubts and build positive social relationships across racial and ethnic lines. This can also help strengthen and stabilize newly diverse neighborhoods and allow residents to enjoy potential benefits.

By supporting affordable housing in your community, you may help a family finally buy their first home. You may be helping children who can now study in their bedrooms. You may be helping someone who wants to correct the mistakes of their past or to seek a better future. All in all, you're helping build a stronger and more vibrant community for everyone in it.

CHAPTER 3

Building a Legacy

I hear all the time how people just want to make enough money to be able to give back. "If I could just win the lottery, I would do such good with it." I think that demonstrates an important point: for many of us, it isn't about the money, but instead, about what good we can do with that money.

What good do you want to do? What amazing thing would you accomplish or create? Who would you spend your time with if time and money weren't an option?

Time is truly our most valuable asset, and with the time we have on earth, what we accomplish on that journey is what determines whether we have a legacy to leave behind.

What will your legacy be?

When you've passed on and people speak your name, what will they say? Will you be proud of what you are currently leaving behind? Or are you wanting something more?

Take time in this chapter to put your legacy in writing and to determine your "why"—your driving force behind why you do what you do.

Is it about paying off that debt? Or is it about paying off the debt so you don't have to go to a 9-to-5 job to cover your expenses so that you can spend your days being with the people you love doing things you enjoy?

Our legacy is our time stamp on life. It's what we give to the world to make it a better place. Think about these questions and create your own here and now. What is your legacy? What is your why?

Figuring Out Your Why

_____

_____

_____

_____

_____

_____

Building a Legacy

Housing For Purpose

CHAPTER 4

Introduction to Real Estate Investing

- **We look for <u>large properties</u> (Minimum of 3 bedrooms/2 bathrooms)**
- **<u>In good neighborhoods</u> (low crime rate, good schools, close to public transportation)**
- **That are <u>appreciating</u> (growth opportunity and source of OPM is property gains equity),**
- **<u>Located in unrestricted areas</u> (to minimize restrictions and hoops to jump through)**
- **That can or are already <u>cash flowing</u> (so we can profit whether we have one resident or several).**

If you don't have a basic understanding of how to invest in real estate on the buy side, I encourage you to get in touch with me or to attend one of my **education courses** that better explains the opportunities in real estate, as well as the processes of purchasing an investment property, whether you have the money or not. I will have a resources page at the end of this book on how you can get in touch with me so you're able to get educated in real estate investing and housing for purpose. In the meantime, this chapter gives you a rundown.

What you'll want to better understand are types of properties:

- Single-family homes
- Multi-family housing
- Mobile homes
- Commercial real estate

Each one can be used for a social housing model, but knowing the laws surrounding each type of property and how to run your numbers on the different types of assets is key to making sure you aren't overpaying for a property. While our mission is to help people, end homelessness, and do a good deed, the business side has to make sense. So, acquiring the asset itself at the right price and understanding the legalities behind conducting business in each type of property is crucial.

Introduction to Real Estate Investing

You'll also want to better understand the creative ways we can buy a property:

- Traditional mortgage
- Cash or credit
- Private or hard money
- Owner financing
- Lease options
- Non-profit sources such as crowdfunding, grants, and donations

In the courses I teach, I better explain the mindset behind investing in real estate and the types of properties we want to look for, how to find them, and how to fund them. There are so many resources available to fund the social housing types of deals, but you must understand how real estate investing works before jumping into this strategy. As with any investment, this involves risk, so being aware of those risks and your risk tolerance is very important.

Once we learn how to purchase the property at a discount in the right neighborhood with proper zoning and accommodations in a financially responsible way, we can then drill down into what type of home we want to provide.

Will we help homeless veterans? the formerly incarcerated? children? single moms? These are all things I can coach you on. Once we get specific with your personal plan, we can then continue the process of promoting your mission to receive applications.

Some housing providers want to operate as a nonprofit, instead of as a business, so you will need to better understand the differences between these types of entities. You'll want to have an attorney and tax advisor on your team to help you identify your personal risk tolerance, so you know which route to go and which tax benefits you may be able to take advantages of.

Depending on the group of people you want to help, there may be incentives offered to control real estate markets and redirect development toward needs rather than profits. From securing a percentage of affordable units, to offering zones of areas to encourage the construction of rental properties, governments can play a key role in helping regulate and supervise opportunities to provide decent, affordable housing. At its peak, the right to housing is about living with dignity, feeling secure and safe, and about living a life we all deserve to live.

Common Questions

- Can I do this in my market?
- How and where do I get the money?
- How much time is involved?
- Are there rules or restrictions?
- Do I need to be a nonprofit?
- What if people don't want your type of property in their neighborhood?

CHAPTER 5

Housing as a Business

Owning real estate is one piece of the puzzle with housing for purpose, but you're also conducting a business within the real estate. It's crucial that we understand the different types of properties and the possibilities with each of them.

Two Main Reasons People Get Into Social Housing:

1. **To Maximize Profit**
   (Get into deals with "OPM", known as Other People's Money, higher cash flow, potential for infinite returns, tax benefits.)

2. **To Help People**
   (By providing housing or support on the surface and to provide creative financing strategies for residents to obtain home ownership.)

Depending on the population you choose to help and how educated you are in real estate investing, you can take advantage of both.

Types of Properties

Having a basic understanding of how real estate works is essential to creating beautiful, sustainable housing. Let's take a look at the different types of properties.

- Single-family homes
- Multi-family housing
- Mobile homes
- Commercial real estate

Each one can be used for a social housing model. You may acquire one single family home that has multiple bedrooms, and you can rent out each room. Another approach is to put multiple beds in each room to rent out each bed.

Depending on the size of the property, it may or may not be big enough to fit more than one bed in each room. Bunk beds are fine if the space makes the most sense for it. Some housing providers allow for one person to a room as opposed to multiple people, but it depends on whether you want individuals having their own room and if the business model allows for it on the financial side.

On the other hand, you may acquire a multi-family property where you can rent out each unit or each bedroom in each unit to those needing a safe place to live.

Unless the housing organization provides co-ed housing or works with the LBGTQ community, we generally like to keep women with women and men with men when it comes to rooming. Part of addiction involves what is called codependency, and it's in the resident's best interest to be able to recover without distractions or potential relapses.

If you were to provide housing for both, it's probably safer to have men in a separate unit within the complex than the women, as opposed to renting one unit to both a man and woman.

There are lots of different ways to get creative on the type of housing.

Knowing whether there are zoning restrictions, local or county requirements, and what each neighborhood allows or prohibits will help you make a better investment decision, because all of these things matter when it comes to developing your shared housing model. While many of the individuals we house may be a part of a protected class, cities may be able to put restrictions or enforce moratoriums on where you can have these homes.

Purchasing a Property

Buying a property can be done several different ways.

- Traditional mortgage
- Cash or credit
- Private or hard money
- Owner financing
- Lease options
- Non-profit sources such as crowdfunding

Purchasing a property traditionally through a bank can be a simple way to do it, but this is considered an investment property, not a personal residence. This means the financing terms may or may not permit you to purchase a home traditionally for investment use.

When we are purchasing properties as investments, we may need to get more creative, like purchasing with commercial mortgages instead of residential, or buying using private money loans versus traditional mortgages.

Sometimes, we don't even own the properties we use for our specialized housing, but instead, we rent them from someone else or do what's called a lease option, in which we lease the property for a period with the option to buy it at a later date.

If you intend to create a nonprofit to conduct your social housing strategy, you may be permitted to tap into funding that people who do it as a business cannot. For example, nonprofits may be eligible for grants, community development funding and any other not-for-profit type of funding.

The Small Business Administration often has money available for start-up businesses, but it all depends on the business structure.

Business structure is very important, so you'll want to make sure you consult with an attorney on how you should be structured before purchasing a property.

How Do We Make Money?

The cash flow formula will help you understand the numbers behind making money, but all in all, we operate as a rental property. Where that money comes from depends on the types of people that we are housing and those individuals' personal resources. For example, if you have a veteran renting from you who is on some sort of medical assistance like disability, that may be a funding source to cover their portion of the rent.

We can make money by renting out the rooms or beds per week or per month to individuals in need, or by renting out an entire house to an already existing group or organization who wants a special-use home for their mission.

So, let's do an example.

Let's say you have a property where your monthly payment, including principal, interest, taxes, and insurance, is $1,500 per month. Let's say you have additional expenses, such as property management, utilities, or insurance, of $500 per month. That means each month, your expenses are $2,000 out of pocket.

Now, let's say we have four bedrooms, with two people to a room. Let's say each person pays $800 per month to rent out a bed. That means we are renting to eight people for a total of $6,400, so our monthly income is $6,400.

To determine our cash flow, we would take our total rent minus our payment, minus our expenses. So, $6,400 minus $2,000 is $4,400. That means, the four-bedroom house would have a positive cash flow of $4,400 per month, which is about $52,000 per year.

Please understand, this is rough math and rough numbers to help you better understand the concept.

Depending on your level of support for the housing, your level of management and involvement, and the legal allowance for unrelated people under one roof, these numbers will vary.

Levels of Involvement as Investor (1–4)

**GENERALLY

1. Rent to the individual directly, no staff

2. Rent to the individual directly with house manager as tenant, no hired staff

3. Rent to individual with house manager as tenant and peer support person/property manager as your employee

4. Rent to existing organization and be entirely hands-off

Start thinking about what level you would like to participate at. You can always start at one level and switch to another as your business progresses.

CHAPTER 6

Housing Requirements

Several states operate their homes, whether sober homes or group homes—the type doesn't matter—according to the national standard for recovery homes.

Depending on which state you open your homes in, you may or may not have state standards or restrictions on what you can and cannot do. How many people per room, how many bathrooms per resident, how much storage space each individual needs to have—all those things are regulated by a national alliance, and sometimes even a state alliance.

If you go to **narronline.org**, you'll be able to find more information on national standards and state standards and why this is important.

The whole mission with housing for purpose is to have nice houses in good neighborhoods to contribute to society in a positive way and to help individuals become better. Operating ethically is crucial. The national standard gives a set of guidelines to follow so we can make sure we are doing our best to genuinely help people.

While the certification process is not required in all states, it is something to strive for. If you operate a certified home, your name will be published within the state and national sites. This is a great way to market yourself to future residents and gives you a tremendous amount of credibility.

CHAPTER 7

The Details

Furnishing your properties is an important part to your mission because this a place where you want your residents to feel at peace, to think clearly, and to find security so they can grow in a way that is beneficial to their well-being, their future, and ultimately, to their life. When you provide a safe place to live that gives a sense of feeling at home. You are giving your residents permission to be themselves and to naturally feel inclined to be vulnerable in a way that allows us to see their progression. When you go to furnish your properties, consider the following things:

Bedrooms

Twin XL (minimum size recommended)
Bunk Beds are okay to save space, but not always encouraged
Set of sheets, comforter, and pillow for each bed/resident

Plastic drawers are okay, especially if you have several residents

House manager needs a cabinet with a lock for supplies/medications

Kitchen

Multiple appliances may be required (Example: two refrigerators)
Disposable or plastic dishes and utensils
Toaster, coffee pot, and microwave
Dining table with seating

Living Room

Large couch or multiple couches and chairs to fit all residents at one time

Bathrooms

Plunger
Toilet brush
Space for each residents' toiletries
One bath towel and one wash cloth per resident

Common Area

Computer, printer, and fax
Desk
Chair

Extras

TVs (not required and sometimes discouraged)
Religious/spiritual material (not encouraged for some—revisit your mission statement and target market before providing these types of material)
Reading material
Toiletries
Laundry detergent (Be careful with this one)
Dish soap
Dishes, plastic containers, and pots and pans
Cleaning supplies (Be careful with this one)
Hampers
Motivational wall art
Outdoor Furniture
Rugs
Plants

In my **Housing for Purpose education course**, we go over why we furnish the properties the way we do and offer tips and tricks that may help you in building your first social home. My experience has been that you want to treat each property as if you were to live there yourself. Keep this notion in mind not only as you furnish your properties but also when you purchase them. If it's not a property you'd live in, whether as is or after renovation, and if it's not in a neighborhood you'd feel safe living in, then don't buy it.

Tricks of the Trade

- Accept Donations
- Gently Used Clothing Is Helpful
- Thrift Store Finds Are a Plus
- Toiletries for the First Few Days
- Cheap Bedding
- Storage for Medication
- Plastic or Inexpensive Storage
- Appliances and Space in Fridge for Everyone
- Motivational or Serene Decor
- New Mattresses

CHAPTER 8

Network for Net Worth

No one becomes successful entirely on their own. In this area of real estate, it takes a village to be able to make your business run properly and ethically as well as to be able to provide the resources and support your residents need.

Whether you are brand-new to real estate or to giving back, your team is critical in implementing all your plans.

Who Is on Your Power Team?

For your real estate power team, in order to build your real estate portfolio that will exist as the shelter for your residents, you will need the following:

- **Attorneys**—to make sure you're operating legally and to structure your business or nonprofit entities

- **Realtors**—to help you find properties that meet your needs, to make offers, and to help facilitate parts of your real estate transactions
- **Accountants**—to make sure you are structured to maximize tax benefits in conjunction with your attorney and to assist with your tax filings
- **Contractors**—to help you better understand what needs work on any properties you find and to coordinate and do the physical work necessary to get your properties up and running. They handle all permitting and inspections on your behalf.
- **Property Managers**—to help with managing your homes on the rent collection and repairs side
- **Mortgage Broker**—to help fund your real estate deals and to connect you with other lenders in the industry
- **Community Banker**—to build a local relationship for funding assistance on the real estate side but also on the resident's side so your residents can open local bank accounts from which they can pay rent out of and to which they can receive pay checks
- **Title Company**—will help with all title work regarding your real estate transactions

- **Appraiser**—to value your property so that you can obtain capital based on your net worth and to borrow from the equity within your property, if there is any
- **Mentor**—to guide you on both the real estate investing and social housing aspect of your mission
- **Peer Support**—to help the individuals in your home who need help with financial support or mental support; to be a resource for any assistance in getting a job or finding resources and to be a liaison between you and your residents
- **House Manager**—to hold your residents accountable and to keep everyone in order within the home, leading meetings and support groups and sessions
- **Program Coordinator**—to work as a third-party vendor to your residents outside of housing support. In many cases, there will be requirements to have a Certified Recovery Residence Administrator (CRRA) credential to operate and administer recovery residences, which are sober, safe, and wellness-oriented living environments that promote sustained recovery from substance use conditions. This

is typically a requirement to be a state-certified home.
- **Handyperson**—to make any on-demand necessary minor repairs to assure safety and security within your homes for your residents
- **Counselor/Related Service/Support Groups**—to help your residents recover and have resources to get back on their feet with job placement, mental health assistance such as psychology or therapy sessions, and so on

Each person on your team will play a role in getting your business up and running. Start thinking about your current network of people. Do you have any team members now? What business professionals do you have access to who you think would be a good fit for your mission? Do they have anyone they can put you in contact with to start building your network even more?

Make a list of the key players you already have access to and indicate which part of your business they could add value to.

CHAPTER 9

Marketing Your Mission

As much as we may want to keep our vision quiet, it's important to get your message out there so that you can acquire residents, support, and other people who want to help. When we start getting into the details of our mission, we must consider how we intend to market our message to each resource we are wanting assistance or support from.

For example, if we are looking for residents, we are going to have a different approach and message than if we are looking for people to rent or sell their homes to us. Regardless of which group or person we are marketing to, we need all the following in place:

- **Website**
- **Credentials**
- **Application**
- **House Rules**
- **Code of Ethics**

- **Photos**
- **Contact Information**
- **Testimonials/Reviews/References**
- **Logo**
- **Business Cards**
- **Brochure**
- **Marketing Letter**

Each of the listed bullets play a role with building the foundation of our mission. We need our **website** both on the business side and on the resident side. The website acts a resume not only for people wanting to be involved on the business-to-business, nonprofit-to-nonprofit side, but also to families and people of interest who may want to live in your home under your supervision.

We want to make sure our **credentials** are published on our website for everyone to see. Whether it's certifications we hold, testimonials, reviews, references, honors, or awards, having these credentials in plain sight will help with reputation management as well as on the back end of our site to help with our SEO marketing efforts.

The **application** is mostly for residents and other housing resources to see what requirements are needed to obtain housing, but it's also a great resource to have published on the business-to-business side so they understand what we expect among our residents who wish to live in our homes.

House rules are extremely important. They are going to set the tone for the community within your home and hold your residents accountable. House rules are also part of NARR requirements, so if you abide by their standards and implement the house rules, as they like to see within a recovery home of any sort, you are likely to maintain certifications and all credentials associated with having safely operated and structured homes.

The Code of Ethics referenced in the NARR sections in previous chapters helps us all be mutually accountable and to keep our properties up to a standard that is ethically and morally appealing to anyone looking for a safe place to live. Without a code of ethics, we don't have a standard to follow; without a standard to follow, we must rely heavily on our own moral compass. On the surface, this may seem effortless to many, but as we get into housing and get into profit-sharing opportunities and making money, not everyone can always resist the temptation to be greedy or break the rules. The Code of Ethics is extremely important.

Photos are great because they show real examples of the properties your residents may live in and real photos of a room they may stay in, a kitchen they may eat in and a living room they may gather in. Photos are everything. While we do want to have pictures of properties on our websites, we must be cautious of publishing photos of any people or addresses without their permission. We do not want to put anyone on our website who doesn't permit their photo to be used; otherwise, we may be violating HIPAA laws. We also do not want to publish addresses for the protection and safety of our residents.

When we publish our **contact information**, be sure this is a different address than the residential addresses of our properties. We need a business address or no address at all. The best contact information is a contact form integrated into your website for lead capturing, where we can obtain a potential resident's contact information for future marketing and support services. However, we also want to provide a good working email and phone number for people to reach us directly. If you accept text messages, be sure to indicate that on your contact information page.

One of the best ways to advertise your mission is through word-of-mouth advertising, and this extends into **testimonials, reviews, and references**. Whether its directly posted to your website or on Google, show it on your website in some way. There are widgets and add-ons you can put on your website on the back end to make sure your social media pages and Google or Yelp reviews can be seen right on your webpage.

When you get into the business development side of your mission, your **logo** will be everything. It will be what people remember, what they see, and what they recognize. It will be used in your advertising, potentially on merchandise and other associated marketing material, and it will be what other people promote on your behalf with or without you asking. Make sure your logo is something you intend to keep long-term, because if your brand and mission take off, it will be what people reference. If you have to change it after your business or nonprofit is already well known, it could damage your future branding.

While **business cards** may seem somewhat obsolete, they are still a great networking and marketing piece. These can be simple, complex, printed, or digital. Whatever type you choose, just make sure they have the critical information, including your name, your organization's name, your contact information, and a place to reference your mission, like a website. These are also great decorations at other businesses that have clientele you may be able to house.

A **brochure** can help in providing more information than a business card can, and they are great for mail marketing campaigns or proposals you give to future investors, businesses, nonprofits, and even families of future residents. Make sure you include photos, contact information, and a list of services your organization provides within the brochure.

Lastly, your **marketing letter** is critical because this is what you use to spread your message. You will use this to reach out to potential property owners, potential support groups, potential residents, and other businesses or nonprofits that could be affiliated with your work or who align with your mission. This letter needs to be effective, honest, and grammatically correct. The letter should also include your logo, the name of your organization, and your personal name and contact information. Be sure you sign the letter in your own handwriting and write out the address and return address in your own handwriting—this is a proven personal touch that's recommended.

Examples of basic website:

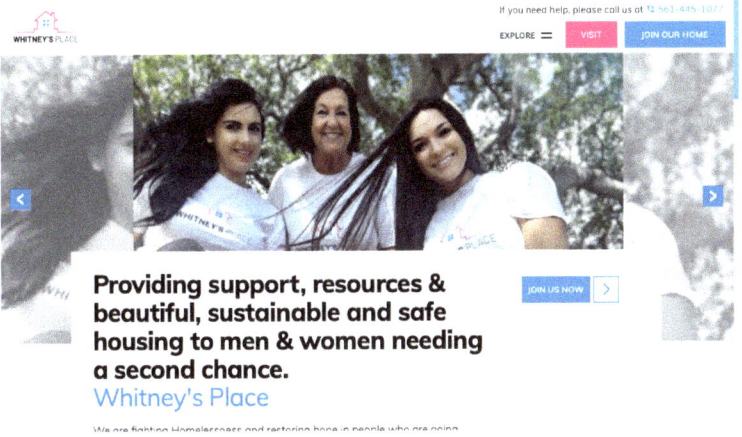

There are many resources out there to help build your website if you aren't tech savvy, and there are apps you can download to have professionals create your website and other marketing materials if you aren't creative either.

Create an account on Fiverr and see if you can find someone to help build your marketing materials.

CHAPTER 10

The Power of Giving Back

Growing up in a small town, you see a lot of struggle. Unfortunately, I had a lot of friends and family who suffered from drug and alcohol addiction. For as long as I can remember, I've always felt compelled to help that particular vulnerable population.

One of the biggest setbacks in my life was when I lost a very good friend to an overdose. It broke me. I suffered from depression from age 21 to about age 24, and it was very difficult. It wasn't until I moved to the Sunshine State that I started to see light at the end of the tunnel.

When I moved to Florida, I began volunteering. I had heard that helping other people can improve your own mental state and well-being, because by giving to others you start to feel grateful for all that you have. I learned this is true.

I was privileged to work with more than fifty-five non-profit organizations across south Florida. It was amazing. But one of the most memorable nonprofits I ever worked with was Place of Hope. Place of Hope is a nonprofit in Palm Beach County, Florida, where they house neglected children and those aging out of foster care.

If you aren't familiar with the foster care system, here's what happens: If you are eighteen years old and you have not yet been adopted, when you turn eighteen, you can age out of the system. That alone can be a tragedy, but what's worse is when an eighteen-year-old has brothers and sisters still in the foster care system. Because what will now happen is either they will be separated from their siblings, or they will take responsibility for them. No boy or girl wants to be separated from the only family they have, and a lot of times, this can lead to homelessness and even human trafficking.

Place of Hope takes all those kids in so that no one has to be separated. I fell in love with this mission, and I told myself that if I ever get to a position to give back financially, Place of Hope would be the first nonprofit I would give back to. By giving to them, I was able to overcome depression.

Fast-forward, I'm in my mid-twenties, and I find myself at a crossroads, like many people do at that time in life.

I disliked working a nine-to-five for someone else. I no longer wanted to ask for permission to have holidays off, weekends off, or birthdays off. I didn't like the idea of someone else controlling my time or money.

When that happened, I decided that it was time to find a new path. And for me, that path was real estate.

I come from a family of investors, developers, and businesspeople, so it was only natural that I would find my way into real estate at some point. However, I didn't learn it from my family. No, no, no. My dad made me get a financial education, because his philosophy was, "What good is it if I give you all the money and give you all the properties? How will you ever be able to stand on your own two feet?" And he was right.

So, when I was twenty-five years old, in February 2016, I quit my job at a car dealership, where I was working to make about $40,000 per year. I had a ton of student loan debt and credit card debt, and I was living off a tax return. I was in a terrible financial position when I started my path with getting a financial education.

I went to a free seminar in a hotel ballroom where the trainer was talking about her lifestyle since she had been investing, and there were three things that really stuck out to me that she had and that I desperately wanted.

Those three things were time, money, and freedom. Not only that, but she was also a stay-at-home mom, which was my lifelong dream.

A week after that free seminar, I went to a three-day training, where I learned more in-depth about real estate strategies and how they could fit into my life. From there, I attended some specialized, advanced, higher-level education courses on specific topics, and that is where the game changed for me.

A few months after attending that training, I was involved in my first investment: a sober home for men in drug and alcohol recovery. This is where my life changed. My mindset changed, my vision changed, my bank account changed, and most importantly, my ability to give on that grander scale changed.

Providing Second Chances

I met men and women, but mostly men, of various ages from all different walks of life. Some were highly educated, some were right out of high school, some were in a transition phase of life, some were exploring their sexuality. Despite their differences, they all had one thing in common: they lacked connection.

Shortly after meeting these men, I took a course on becoming a certified Progressive Recovery Life Coach, and I learned during that course that the opposite of addiction is not necessarily sobriety—it is connection; it is purpose; it's a feeling of belonging and a feeling of being able to contribute to the world in a good way. The people I met who were in early recovery could not see beyond the fences because they were so invested in their artificial high that nothing could give them a natural high.

Something I've always loved to do is to help people feel better about themselves, because although I had experienced my own hardships, I continued to have faith and hope that one day, everything would be all right. Everything would get better. Being able to help other people realize the beauty of life and all that there is to be grateful for was something I knew all too well, and I desperately wanted to contribute more of that to the world.

So, we took this property that needed a little love, and we made it a home for people to find that connection and sense of belonging.

Before:

After:

With just a little paint, grass seed, and paving the driveway, it made one person's trash another person's treasure.

Being a part of this home was the first time I discovered what it's like to truly give unselfishly. I remember like it was yesterday the day I stepped foot into this property and how my mom, our great friend Lynn (who was part owner of the house), and I jumped on the opportunity to decorate it and paint. All the furniture was donated from an estate sale, and we bought brand-new bedding and decorations to make it feel homey.

There were five bedrooms, three bathrooms, and two living rooms in which people could have social gatherings and house meetings.

Each bedroom had closet space and a dresser for each resident. The bathrooms had standing showers and cabinet space for each resident's toothbrush, toothpaste, and other toiletries.

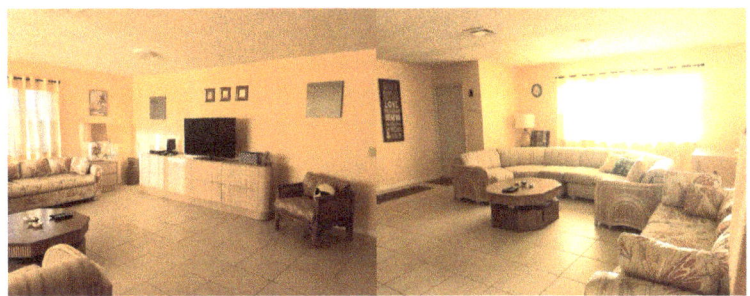

The kitchen had a large table where all the residents could share meals.

The back patio had a beautiful picnic table that Lynn was so excited to contribute for the residents to enjoy in the privacy of the backyard, where they could hang out on beautiful days.

Many times, when someone is in early recovery, the individual is confined to the treatment center and housing provider. They are usually not permitted, or at least not encouraged, to leave the area until they've completed their treatment program. Several of the residents who were out of state could not get home to their families for holidays. So, I would go to the house and cook for the residents. Easter was special because instead of cooking *for* them, I cooked *with* them. We had a former chef in the house who made a delicious carrot dish that I'll never forget.

Making a Difference

While all the details were important, it was the results that were most important.

I built a special relationship with one individual who must remain nameless in this book, but I met him shortly before the opening of this property. He had been addicted to heroin.

We instantly had a platonic connection, almost like a brother-sister connection. I saw so much in him, and he appreciated so much of me. I could see in his eyes that he had a lot of pain and regret. I think he saw the same in mine.

One day, I got a call that he had to be taken to the emergency room for an overdose. A call was made to 911, and he had to receive Narcan basically to come back to life.

I chased him down at the hospital, but he was nowhere to be found. Sometimes, when you're dealing with someone in early recovery, they aren't ready to get sober, and we cannot force them to. He had some hard times trying to get back on his feet. He wasn't ready to give it up.

But a few months later, he came to the house. He was on some sort of drug, standing outside the house in the street and crying. He finally wanted help.

He came inside, still crying, and I held him for a good fifteen minutes in a chair by the window while he sobbed. He confessed his fears, his disappointment in himself, and his love for his mother. His head remained on my chest until a van came to pick him up to take him to treatment. That was in July 2017.

From that point on and still today, he remains clean and sober. He became a father and a husband and is back with his family, living life to the fullest.

I don't tell this story to talk about myself—I tell it because it's stories like this that give people hope. It's homes like the one we built that help people find themselves to make better choices for a greater outcome in life. We cannot force people to change, but we can provide the resources to show them the way so that they, themselves, want and choose to change.

Leaving a Legacy

As a result of learning how to invest in real estate, I've been able to help more people than I had ever imagined, through working with and providing safe housing to people who need it and by sharing my message. It's been a really amazing experience to be able to see lives change for the better.

I became a professional speaker, sharing my story nationwide about how I've used housing for purpose. I've been able to meet so many people who share similar stories and see Real estate investing as their second chance.

And finally, in 2019, because of my financial education, I was able to accomplish the one thing I said I wanted to: I was able to donate $25,000 to Place of Hope. With my $25,000 donation, Place of Hope built a library, filled it with financial education books for all the kids they house (which were also donated on my behalf), and on April 16, 2019, they named the library after me and my family.

If you help enough people get what they want, you'll get what you want every single time.

Conclusion

Real Estate investing is not easy. Housing for purpose is not easy. But our time on earth will pass whether we do something easy or not. Taking life into your own hands and doing more is what this book is about.

We seem to know enough about what needs to be done, but we hardly act on it. We do more talking about it than doing about it, and much of our dreams remain pipe dreams. Putting our vision into action is what will give us the opportunity to create the legacy we've always dreamed of.

When it comes to real estate, part of the problem lies in the lack of financial education – we need financial education to better understand how to overcome the obstacles we may face as investors. We aren't taught basic knowledge on banking, accounting, homeownership, or anything real-estate related in school unless we specialize in it in college. Even then, the information is limited. So, what do you do about that?

I encourage anyone who is considering getting a financial education to do it. Read books. Take a class that will teach you the basics of what you need to know. Watch videos on how deals are structured. Get a mentor who has done what it is you want to do. Whether it's real estate, business, whatever—invest in yourself, because you'll get run over if you just sit there. You've got to act, get up off your assets, and make something happen for yourself. No one is going to do it for you.

When it comes to housing for purpose, housing policies themselves cannot guarantee decent and affordable housing. We, as a people, need to help.

When we all come together to do good, the world becomes a more enjoyable place to live. I don't know how many people will buy this book and read it, and I purposely didn't overwhelm you with education since it can be a lot to take in, but I hope that what I did share of my story is able to help at least one life. Whether it's to follow a dream, to build a house, to overcome depression, to get sober—I'm rooting for you!

Action Plan

TO GET STARTED WITH SOCIAL HOUSING

1. **LOCATE AREA OF INTEREST BASED ON PERSONAL DESIRE/RESEARCH/NEED/ ATTRACTION.**
2. **FIND PROPERTY IN THE AREA OF INTEREST THAT MEETS STANDARDS TO ACCOMDATE DESIRED STRATEGY.**
3. **CROSS-REFERENCE PROPERTY/RUN NUMBERS/DUE DILIGENCE.**
4. **LINE UP GROUPS/RESOURCES/PARTNERS FOR RESIDENTS AND FURNISHINGS.**
5. **AFTER WE'VE CONFIRMED IT'S A DEAL, WE PURCHASE PROPERTY CREATIVELY AT A DISCOUNT.**
6. **START MARKETING.**
7. **RECEIVE AND REVIEW APPLICATIONS/ BOOKINGS.**
8. **ACCEPT APPLICANTS AND START MOVE-IN PROCESS.**

Contact Information

Whitney (Chaffin) Sellers can be reached for correspondence at
info@whitneysplace.org

To get educated or for more information on personal mentorship with Whitney, please contact me.

On Instagram:
@whit.sellers
@whitneysplaces

On TikTok:
@whitneychaffin

www.ingramcontent.com/pod-product-compliance
Ingram Content Group UK Ltd.
Pitfield, Milton Keynes, MK11 3LW, UK
UKHW020247240426
12048UKWH00027B/1648